Contents

*Any words appearing in the text in bold, **like this**, are explained in the Glossary.*

What is a tornado?

Tornadoes are among the most terrifying forces of nature. A tornado is a fast-moving, spinning column of air that twists down from a thundercloud. The twisting column of air reaches all the way down to the ground from the cloud in a **funnel**. Many tornadoes look like high, narrow black spinning tops. Other tornadoes look like incredibly long twisted ropes, or even bubbling masses of clouds.

Most of the tornadoes that happen are small. They may last for only a few seconds and do no damage at all. Large tornadoes can be hundreds of metres wide and kilometres high. These tornadoes are the most violent winds on Earth.

This is a picture of a typical tornado. Tornadoes are often called twisters, because of the way the winds within them twist and spin.

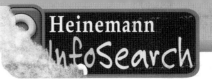
Heinemann
InfoSearch

Terrifying Tornadoes

Louise and Richard Spilsbury

Spilsbury, Louis

Terrifying
tornadoes /
Louise and

J551.
553

1551439

First published in Great Britain by
Heinemann Library, Halley Court,
Jordan Hill, Oxford OX2 8EJ, part of
Harcourt Education.
Heinemann is a registered trademark of
Harcourt Education Ltd.

© Harcourt Education Ltd 2004
First published in paperback in 2005
The moral right of the proprietor has been
asserted.

Editorial: Andrew Farrow and Dan Nunn
Design: David Poole and Paul Myerscough
Illustrations: Geoff Ward
Picture Research: Rebecca Sodergren and
Debra Weatherley
Production: Viv Hichens

Originated by Dot Gradations Limited
Printed in China by WKT Company Limited

ISBN 0 431 17837 2 (hardback)
08 07 06 05 04
10 9 8 7 6 5 4 3 2 1

ISBN 0 431 17865 8 (paperback)
09 08 07 06 05
10 9 8 7 6 5 4 3 2 1

**British Library Cataloguing in
Publication Data**
Spilsbury, Richard, 1963 –
Terrifying tornadoes. – (Awesome forces
of nature)
1. Tornadoes – Juvenile literature
I. Title II. Spilsbury, Louise
551.5'53
A full catalogue record for this book is
available from the British Library.

Acknowledgements
The publishers would like to thank the
following for permission to reproduce
photographs:

AFP pp. **21** (Arko Datta-STR), **23** (Hector
Mata-STF), **27** (Steve Schaefer-STR);
Associated Press pp. **16** (Handout), **19**
(Rahman), **20** (Carter), **26** (Schiappa); NOAA
pp. **4**, **6**, **7**, **9**, **12**, **25**; Oxford Scientific
Films pp. **15** (Faidley), **17** (Faidley); Photo
Library p. **28** (Fema); Popperfoto p. **10**
(Doherty); Rex Features pp. **5** (Houston
Post), **14** (Houston Post); Science Photo
Library p. **24** (Menzel).

Cover photograph reproduced courtesy of
Getty Images/Taxi.

Spinning winds

Tornadoes can travel at great speeds and they can cause terrible destruction. The spinning winds in the funnel of a tornado act like an enormous vacuum cleaner. They can suck up cars, trains, trees and even houses and drop them down again from a great height. The winds in tornadoes spin so fast that they can tear buildings apart and flatten whole forests when they pass over.

Where did tornadoes get their name?

The word 'tornado' comes from the Latin word *tonare* or the Spanish word *tornar*, which mean 'to twist or turn'. It may also come from the Spanish word *tronada*, which means thunderstorm. These words give a good description of tornadoes – twisting thunderstorms.

When a series of tornadoes hit Houston, Texas, USA, in November 1992, many homes and buildings were severely damaged.

What causes tornadoes?

Tornadoes happen when warm, wet winds from one direction meet colder, dryer winds moving in the opposite direction. When these two kinds of winds meet, the warm air rises over the cold air and starts to spin. This is how a tornado starts.

The rising, spinning air sucks in warm air from just above the ground. This warm air becomes part of the tornado. Warm air rises and this makes the tornado rise higher in the air. As it rises, it spins faster and faster. This spiralling part is called the **funnel** or spout.

TORNADO ⚡ FACTS

! The winds spinning in the funnel of a big tornado may blow faster than any other winds on Earth.

! Two out of every hundred tornadoes have spinning winds of over 330 kilometres per hour.

In this picture, the black column of twisting air is the part of a tornado we call the funnel.

What is a tornado like?

A tornado may spin for just a few seconds, or it may go on for several hours. It may spin over one spot for a while and then suddenly dart off in one direction. It is very difficult to tell where a tornado is going next. Sometimes they zigzag about, moving quickly from side to side. Sometimes there are several tornadoes that move in a group or follow each other.

What is the difference between a tornado and a hurricane?

Tornadoes and **hurricanes** both have spinning winds, but they are very different forces of nature. A hurricane is a huge storm, but a tornado comes from a storm. Tornadoes can happen in hurricanes. Although they are violent, tornadoes are only very small compared to hurricanes. Tornadoes almost always start far inland, away from the coast. Hurricanes start over warm oceans. Most tornadoes last for less than half an hour, while hurricanes can rage for weeks.

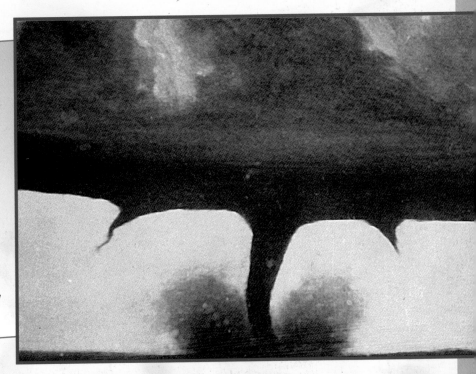

Some tornadoes grow so big that they create other smaller tornadoes. These extra tornadoes can head off on their own. This picture shows the oldest known photo of a group of tornadoes. It was taken in 1884!

What is a tornado's eye?

The **eye** is the very centre of a tornado. The eye is the point around which the strong tornado winds spiral and twist. It is calm inside the eye. There may be a few clouds and just a gentle breeze. People who have lived through a tornado describe its sound as being like the roaring of many trains or the buzzing of millions of bees. In the eye it may suddenly become quieter.

Some people have seen inside a tornado's eye. They say that when you look up it is like standing at the bottom of a huge pipe. The sides look like a stack of huge, ring-shaped clouds. These clouds are so thick that you cannot see through them.

This diagram shows the speeds in different parts of a tornado as it travels across the ground.

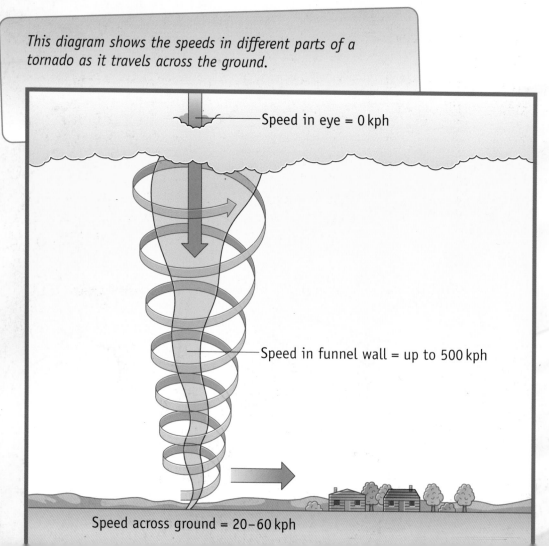

Speed in eye = 0 kph

Speed in funnel wall = up to 500 kph

Speed across ground = 20–60 kph

What is a waterspout?

Most tornadoes happen far inland, away from water. A waterspout is an unusual tornado that forms over an area of water, such as a river, lake or ocean. This kind of tornado sucks up water as well as warm air.

Waterspouts can be one metre to tens of metres thick. They can be as little as 10 metres high, but the largest waterspout ever seen was over 1500 metres high! Waterspouts usually only last for about 15 minutes. They don't cause as much destruction as tornadoes, but they can seriously damage ships that meet them at sea.

It's raining fish and toads!

Like tornadoes on land, waterspouts pick up objects and drop them down again. Waterspouts have caused showers of toads in France, have dropped tadpoles in New York and once dropped fish from the skies over Rhode Island in the USA!

This is a waterspout off Florida Keys, USA. Most waterspouts look something like this – their thin column-shaped funnels sucking water up in the air.

Where and when do tornadoes happen?

Tornadoes can happen anywhere in the world, if the right combination of warm, damp winds meet colder, dryer winds. More tornadoes happen in the USA than anywhere else in the world. Tornadoes also happen in Australia, parts of Europe, such as Italy and the UK, and in Bangladesh and India.

Tornadoes in England!

On average, about 30 tornadoes are reported in the UK each year. Most happen around East Anglia, southern England and the Midlands. On 21 November 1981, a total of 105 tornadoes were reported. This is the highest number of tornadoes to hit any country in Europe in a single day. They happened in the area between Gwynedd, Essex and Humberside and thirteen were reported in Norfolk alone. Fortunately, none of the tornadoes were big or fast enough to do too much damage.

These firemen are making the roof of this home in Bognor Regis, in the UK, safe after it was damaged by a tornado in 1981. As well as damaging buildings, the tornado also injured several people in the town.

The reason that most tornadoes happen in parts of the USA is the Rocky Mountains! Cool, dry air heading down from Canada is sent eastwards when it hits the huge wall formed by the Rocky Mountains. This cool air then blows over the flat open stretch of land known as the Great Plains. Here it crashes into patches of warm, damp air travelling up from the Gulf of Mexico. Tornadoes are so common in this area that it has become known as 'Tornado Alley'.

TORNADO ⚡ FACTS

! The USA has about 100,000 thunderstorms a year, which cause between 800 and 1000 tornadoes a year.

! In the USA more than 80 people are killed by tornadoes every year.

! The Great Plains area in the USA has seven out of ten of all the tornadoes that happen on Earth!

This map of the world shows where the world's worst tornadoes happen.

Asia

North America

Europe

Atlantic Ocean

Tornado Alley

Africa

South America

Indian Ocean

Australia

Pacific Ocean

KEY
Tornado areas

Antarctica

When do tornadoes happen?

In the right wind and weather conditions, tornadoes can appear at any time of the day or night. Most tornadoes, however, start in the afternoon or early evening. This is the time of day when the Sun has warmed up the ground and the air above it. This produces the hot air that is needed to create a tornado.

Tornadoes can also happen at any time of the year, although in many areas they are more common at some times of the year than others. These times are known as **tornado seasons**. In Tornado Alley and much of the southern USA, the tornado season happens in spring and summer. Further north, tornadoes tend to come later in the year.

Dimmit, Texas is in Tornado Alley. This tornado, which hit the area on 2 June 1995, was so strong that it ripped up roads and pavements. It carried cars hundreds of metres before destroying them.

Tri-state Twisters, USA, 1925

The Tri-state Twisters were a terrible series of tornadoes that hit the USA on 18 March 1925. The tornadoes came in so close to the ground that people could not see them coming. They looked like big rolling clouds. The twisters raged through three states – Missouri, Indiana and Illinois – at over 100 kilometres per hour, following a ridge where many mining towns were built.

The Tri-state Twisters were very wide and brought terrible winds and heavy downpours of rain. They wrecked trees, farmland and buildings. They killed 695 people and injured over 2000. One town, Gorham, in Illinois, was totally destroyed and more than half of the population were killed or injured.

This map shows you the path of destruction followed by the Tri-state Twisters. This set of tornadoes was one of the worst in America's history. They lasted for three-and-a-half hours and finally broke up north-east of Princeton in Indiana.

KEY
■ Path of tornadoes

What happens in a tornado?

People cannot always see the twisting tail of a tornado to tell them danger is on the way. Low storm clouds often hide approaching tornado storms. The first signs that a tornado is coming may be that the sky turns a dark green colour or big hailstones fall from the clouds. If you can hear a sound like a rushing waterfall or a roaring jet engine then the tornado is getting very close.

TORNADO ⚡ FACTS

! A tornado moves like a spinning top. The winds in the **funnel** spin round and round at the same time as the tornado travels across a stretch of land.

! The winds in the funnel of a tornado can spin at speeds of over 500 kilometres per hour.

! A tornado can rush across the ground at up to 65 kilometres per hour, as fast as a moving car.

Some people think they can outrun tornadoes in their cars. But tornadoes can travel fast and they can toss cars about or roll them over and over as if they were toys.

How do tornado winds cause damage?

Tornado winds break things up and toss them around. Many of the people killed in tornadoes die when objects that are thrown through the air hit them. These winds can blow over walls, mobile homes, cars and trains and they can snap overhead cables and **power lines**, which can be very dangerous. Broken power lines can **electrocute** people or sparks from them may start fires.

The winds in the funnel of a tornado have incredibly powerful **suction**. Tornadoes can suck up anything, including millions of tonnes of dust, soil, sand or roof tiles. They drop them elsewhere when the tornado weakens. When soil and gravel are blown about by tornadoes they cause damage when people breathe them in or get them in their eyes. They can blow against things with such force that they act like sandpaper. They also clog up and **pollute** reservoirs and rivers.

Tornado winds move objects so fast that when they crash into something or someone they can cause serious harm. Even small objects, like this fork that has been embedded into a tree, can do a lot of damage.

Tornado strength

The strength of a tornado is judged by its wind speeds. Wind speeds are worked out from the amount of damage that they cause. It is too difficult and dangerous to measure them as they happen. The winds are often so strong that they destroy measuring equipment!

F-0 to F-1 tornadoes cause light to moderate damage to trees and buildings. They break off branches and knock down chimneys. They may also blow mobile homes over.

F-2 to F-3 tornadoes cause serious damage. They can tear the roofs off houses, lift and toss cars and overturn trains.

F-4 and F-5 tornadoes are the most violent winds on Earth. They can rip bark off trees, lift and carry whole buildings and throw cars over 100 metres! F-5 tornadoes usually occur only every other year in the USA.

The 'F' used to indicate tornado strengths stands for 'Fujita'. This is because the scale is named after the scientist who created it, Dr Tetsuya Fujita. Dr Fujita is pictured here, studying a mini-tornado created in his laboratory.

What is a tornado storm like?

The storms that produce tornadoes bring heavy showers of rain, thunder and lightning with them. Some have even dropped hailstones as big as tennis balls from the sky! Big hailstones like this can cause a lot of damage when they come crashing down to Earth.

When do tornadoes die?

Tornadoes usually break up when they go over colder ground or when the storm clouds above them break up. Most tornadoes only last about 20 minutes and travel less than 25 kilometres. However, some huge tornadoes have travelled 160 kilometres before dying.

Flying cows!

People have told stories of many strange things happening during tornadoes. Hens have had feathers plucked from their backs. Cows have been lifted up, mooing, and dropped down safely far away from their own field. One tornado lifted a pram high in the air and dropped it down again without waking the baby sleeping inside!

Imagine seeing huge hailstones like these falling from the sky towards you! These hailstones fell in Texas, USA.

Bangladesh, 1996

At lunchtime on 13 May 1996 in the Tangail district, north-western Bangladesh, the wind suddenly calmed and it got unbearably hot. Then hailstones the size of tennis balls fell from the sky as huge thunderstorms built up. These thunderstorms produced a series of terrible and destructive tornadoes. The tornadoes ripped bark from trees, uprooted large trees and caused many buildings to collapse.

Many people in Bangladesh are quite poor and their houses are not very strong. Many houses were built on hillsides out of reach of the floods that often happen during the **monsoon**, the country's wettest season. These houses were hit by the strongest winds.

'The whole village has been reduced to a vast grave.' A police officer in Bashail, one of the villages affected

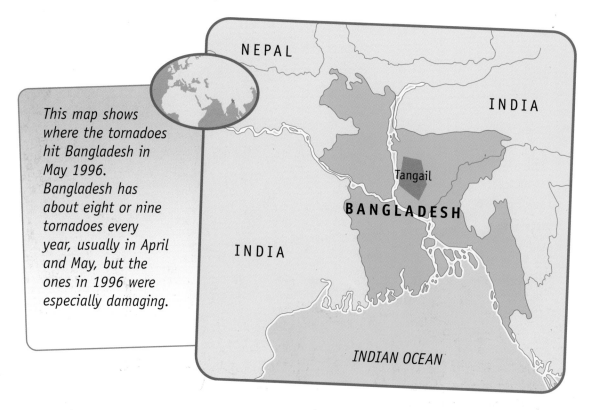

This map shows where the tornadoes hit Bangladesh in May 1996. Bangladesh has about eight or nine tornadoes every year, usually in April and May, but the ones in 1996 were especially damaging.

Many people had built houses from thin sheets of metal. The tornado broke these up and threw the pieces about. The sharp metal pieces whirled in the air and injured many people. The bad weather and poor roads made it very difficult for rescuers to get to many of the villages. In some villages there were no trucks or buses. People had to carry injured friends and neighbours on their backs or in carts. Because of this, it was a long time before many injured people reached hospitals that could help them. By then their injuries had become infected and many died.

The tornadoes lasted about 2 hours and travelled over 25 kilometres. They left a path of destruction nearly 1.5 kilometres wide.

More than 80 villages and 10,000 homes were destroyed by the 1996 tornadoes in Bangladesh. More than 1000 people were killed and 30,000 people were injured.

Who helps after a tornado?

Imagine the scene after a tornado. Houses have collapsed and there is rubbish and **debris** strewn everywhere. Trees have been blown like matchsticks onto roads and buildings. The first people to arrive on a scene like this are rescue workers. They rescue people from cars, mobile homes and crushed houses.

Ambulances and medical workers arrive fast too. They give **first aid** to people who are injured and take those with more serious injuries straight to hospital. Some people will have dust in their eyes or throats which could make them ill. Flying debris may have injured others. Workers from **aid organizations** such as the Red Cross soon arrive. They provide people with the basics – food, clothing and **shelter**. They also provide food and drink to rescue workers.

Rescue workers may use their hands, spades, chainsaws or bulldozers to clear bits of wreckage to reach people who are trapped beneath it.

Finding loved ones

Aid organizations such as the Red Cross help people from other places find out if relatives in the tornado-hit area are safe and well. They also help families who were apart when the tornado hit to find each other again.

Clearing up

One of the biggest jobs after a tornado is clearing up the mess. Broken toys, furniture, clothing, fence posts, glass and crockery are strewn everywhere. Homeowners, **volunteers** and the Army or **National Guard** may all help. It can take weeks or months just to clear up the debris. When the rubble has been cleared, workers can mend or rebuild homes.

*When a tornado hits a **developing country**, people may not have enough money to rebuild their homes or businesses. As well as providing **aid** in the form of food and shelter, aid organizations may also supply tools or other equipment so that people can work and earn money again.*

Oklahoma City, USA, 1999

In 1999, a tornado **swarm** ripped through the US states of Oklahoma and Kansas on Monday afternoon and Tuesday morning of 3–4 May. There were over 70 tornadoes in total. They raged across the land for over 4 hours. At least one of the tornadoes measured 1.5 kilometres across. Winds in some of the tornadoes blew faster than 300 kilometres per hour!

Cars and trucks were thrown around, trees and **power lines** were snapped and buildings were reduced to rubble. In Oklahoma City, an area called Moore was almost completely flattened. In total, thousands of houses were destroyed and 45 people were killed.

'It looks like a bomb hit here. Houses are just levelled [flattened]. It looks like a battlefield.' John Ireland, a resident of Moore

This map shows where tornadoes hit Oklahoma in May 1999.

Who helped in Oklahoma City?

Early TV and radio warnings meant that fewer people died in the disaster than would have been expected. However, many people still needed help. Rescue workers began searching the rubble for survivors straight away. They used dogs to sniff out where people were trapped. Then they used heavy machinery to lift away wrecked building parts. The American Red Cross set up **shelters** for people who had fled their homes or been rescued to spend the night in.

In the weeks after the tragedy, the government provided extra money to create temporary jobs for people whose factories or businesses had been destroyed. They also loaned money to many families so that they could afford to rebuild their homes.

*Hundreds of ordinary people gave money, tins of food, clothes and toiletry items (such as toothbrushes and towels) to an **aid fund**. This helped people who had lost their homes and all their belongings.*

Can tornadoes be predicted?

It is very hard to tell when a tornado will happen. Often, giant storms that seem likely to create a tornado do not, and small storms that do not usually produce a tornado do! However, scientists are working on ways of spotting tornadoes early so that they can warn people to get out of the way.

Weather reports

Weather forecasters can tell where storms are gathering and this helps to predict where tornadoes may start. They study pictures taken by **satellites** far above the Earth. These show where swirling clouds and thunderstorms are growing. They also get reports about storms from weather stations that operate in countries all over the world. In some countries there are groups of **volunteers** who watch out for tornadoes and phone weather stations as soon as they see signs of one.

Scientists use weather balloons like this to work out the direction and speed of the wind, high up in the air. This is one of the pieces of the puzzle they put together to work out when a tornado might happen.

Using advanced technology

Scientists use new technology as well as observing the weather to spot tornadoes early. **Doppler radar** is a special piece of equipment that can tell when there are strong spinning winds in a storm. These are the kinds of strong winds that might become a tornado. Scientists also use equipment that can **detect** lightning flashes between clouds even during daylight. They have worked out that faster flashing means a storm is getting worse.

Who are storm chasers?

Storm chasers are scientists who find and follow storms. They travel in vehicles with special equipment inside, such as video cameras and computers. They use this equipment to study how tornadoes behave. The information they collect is very useful for working out what to expect from future tornadoes.

*Storm chasers try to get as close to the **funnel** of a tornado as they can in order to study it. It is dangerous work and they have to be very careful.*

Can people prepare for tornadoes?

Only a small number of tornadoes actually hit people's homes every year, so it is very unlikely that even people in Tornado Alley will be affected. However, people who live in areas where tornadoes do happen can take steps to protect themselves.

Can buildings be made stronger?

People can make their buildings stronger and better able to resist tornadoes. They can bolt buildings to firm **foundations** and seal the gaps under roof tiles so winds cannot get underneath them. Many people build special **storm cellars**. These are either basements that are strengthened with concrete and strong doors, or separate rooms under the ground in the garden. People can hide in these during a tornado to be safe.

*This is a storm cellar. If people do not have a cellar like this, they should **shelter** in a room on the lowest floor of the house. They should keep away from windows and hide under something to protect themselves from flying **debris**.*

Tornado plans

People should not worry about tornadoes, but they should know what to do if one happens. In the USA, if a 'tornado watch' is announced it means that there is a possibility of a tornado and people should be ready to move to a safe shelter or **evacuate**. A 'tornado warning' means that a tornado has been spotted and people should run to their shelter immediately. Everyone in the family should learn exactly where to go and what to do.

Disaster supplies kit

People in tornado zones are also advised to prepare an emergency kit. This should contain:

- a **first-aid** kit
- a battery-powered radio (as electricity supplies may be cut off)
- a torch (and extra batteries)
- bottled water
- cans and packets of food (and a can opener!)

Local weather stations issue warnings about tornadoes. They send the warnings out as soon as they can on all radio and TV stations in the danger area.

Can tornadoes be prevented?

Tornadoes are natural forces that cannot be stopped. The only things people can do to reduce the damage tornadoes cause are to predict them earlier and be better prepared.

At the moment, only about half of all tornadoes can be spotted in time to warn people about them. In the future, scientists hope to set up systems across the world that can more accurately predict tornadoes. They are also working on ways to stop tornadoes forming. For example, people have tried firing **dry ice** into growing storms. The idea is to make the storm drop more rain, which makes it weaker. In this way scientists might be able to stop a storm producing any full-blown tornadoes.

*In order to reduce the amount of damage tornadoes can do, people need to understand what tornadoes are. This **volunteer** for the US organization **FEMA** is advising a local resident on what to do in the event of a tornado.*

Terrifying tornadoes of the recent past

4 January 1951, Comoro Island

The island of Comoro off eastern Africa was hit by a strong tornado. About 500 people were killed and the city of Anjouan was flattened.

19 April 1963, India and Bangladesh

A tornado travelling at 80 kilometres per hour touched down in India and passed through southern Bangladesh. In India, 139 people were killed and even more died in Bangladesh. People were picked up and thrown 300 to 600 metres.

Midwestern USA, 1965

On 11 April 1965, about 48 tornadoes crashed through the US states of Iowa, Wisconsin, Illinois, Michigan, Indiana and Ohio within a period of 12 hours. These tornadoes killed 256 people and caused more than $200 million of damage.

Dhaka, Bangladesh, 1969

Many people live in the city of Dhaka. When a tornado hit the city on 14 April 1969 it killed 50 people and injured 4000 more.

Midwestern USA, 1974

On 3 and 4 April 1974, 148 tornadoes raged for over 16 hours across the centre of the USA through thirteen states, including Ohio and Kansas. Over 330 people were killed and around 5500 people were injured.

Wichita Falls, Texas, USA, 1979

On 10 April 1979, three tornadoes killed 40 people and injured about 1700 more as they travelled across the US states of Texas and Oklahoma. Shopping **malls** and several hundred buildings were destroyed.

Midwestern USA, 1990

Around 50 tornadoes hit the midwestern USA within 4 hours. They killed 13 people and damaged 24 cities, within 7 states, from Wisconsin to Kansas.

Glossary

aid help given as money, medicine, food or other essential items

aid fund collection of money donated by ordinary people and used to provide aid

aid organizations groups of people who work together to raise money and to provide help for people in need

debris loose bits of solid material, such as stones and rocks

detect spot or find

developing country one of the poorer countries of the world that are gradually trying to develop better conditions for their people

Doppler radar special machine that uses invisible rays to detect where things are

dry ice frozen carbon dioxide. Carbon dioxide is a normal part of our earth's atmosphere. It is the gas that we exhale during breathing and the gas that plants use in photosynthesis.

electrocute kill by electric shock

evacuate when people move from a dangerous place to somewhere they will be safe

eye calm centre of a tornado (or hurricane)

FEMA stands for 'Federal Emergency Management Agency'. FEMA is an American government agency that is in charge of helping people before and after a disaster.

first aid first medical help given to injured people

foundations solid base upon which a building is built

funnel spiralling central part of a tornado

hurricane wind storms that are rather like tornadoes. Hurricanes are bigger and last longer than tornadoes and they start over warm oceans.

malls shopping centres

monsoon wet season in parts of Asia and elsewhere

National Guard volunteer soldiers recruited and trained by each US state. They serve during emergencies and in times of war.

pollute when part of the natural environment is poisoned or harmed by human activity

power lines main cables that carry electricity

satellite object that goes around the Earth in space. Satellites do jobs such as sending out TV signals or taking photographs.

shelter somewhere warm and safe to stay

storm cellar underground room where people can shelter during a bad storm, such as a tornado

suction sucking power

swarm group of tornadoes

tornado season time of the year when tornadoes happen most often

volunteers people who work without being paid for what they do

Find out more

Books

Wild Weather: Thunderstorm, Catherine Chambers (Heinemann Library, 2002)

DK Eyewitness Guides: Hurricane and Tornado, Jack Challoner (Dorling Kindersley, 2000)

DK Guide to Weather, Michael Allaby (Dorling Kindersley, 2000)

Storms, Mark Maslin (Hodder Children's Books, 2000)

Hurricanes and Tornadoes, Neil Morris (Crabtree Pub Co., 1998)

Websites

www.fema.gov/kids/tornado.htm – this website contains facts about tornado dangers, what to do and how to prepare.

www.nationalgeographic.com/eye/tornadoes/tornadoes.html – here you can see video reports from people who have lived through tornadoes.

Disclaimer

All the Internet addresses (URLs) given in this book were valid at the time of going to press. However, due to the dynamic nature of the Internet, some addresses may have changed, or sites may have changed or ceased to exist since publication. While the author and publishers regret any inconvenience this may cause readers, no responsibility for any such changes can be accepted by either the author or the publishers.

Index